First English translation copyright © 2025 by Skyhorse Publishing, Inc.
Published by arrangement with Loewe Verlag GmbH.

Title of the original German edition: *Mein Körper gehört mir-auch im Sport!*
© 2023 Loewe Verlag GmbH, Bindlach

All rights reserved. No part of this book may be reproduced in any manner
without the express written consent of the publisher, except in the case of brief
excerpts in critical reviews or articles. All inquiries should be addressed to Sky
Pony Press, 307 West 36th Street, 11th Floor, New York, NY 10018.

Sky Pony Press books may be purchased in bulk at special discounts for sales
promotion, corporate gifts, fund-raising, or educational purposes. Special
editions can also be created to specifications. For details, contact the Special
Sales Department, Sky Pony Press, 307 West 36th Street, 11th Floor, New York,
NY 10018 or info@skyhorsepublishing.com.

Sky Pony® is a registered trademark of Skyhorse Publishing, Inc.®, a Delaware
corporation.

Visit our website at www.skyponypress.com.

10 9 8 7 6 5 4 3 2 1

Manufactured in China, April 2025
This product conforms to CPSIA 2008

Library of Congress Cataloging-in-Publication Data is available on file.

Cover design by Ramona Karl & Kai Texel
Cover illustrations by Nikolai Renger
US Edition edited by Nicole Frail

Print ISBN: 978-1-5107-7717-0
Ebook ISBN: 978-1-5107-8279-2

Creating a Safe Space in Sports

Preventing Abuse and Taking Care of Our Bodies—and Our Teammates

Written by
Dagmar Geisler

Illustrated by
Nikolai Renger

Translated by
Andy Berasaluce

Afterword by
Alexandra Ndolo
Professional Athlete

Sky Pony Press
New York

Contents

A New Coach   2

Great Talent   5

Such a Strange Feeling   9

Nora Wants the Ground to Swallow Her Up   14

A Dark Cloud   19

Pretty Brave   22

What We Want to Know   24

Information Centers   36

Afterword   38

About the Authors   39

A New Coach

"I'm super excited," says Emilia. "Next week is the state championship and we've never been as good as we are now."

"Mmhhmm," says Nora, not looking happy at all. "What's the matter with you?" Emilia asks. "If anyone should be happy, it's you! In the end, you're better than the rest of us."

That's true. Nora is really good at gymnastics. It's what she has the most fun doing. Especially back handsprings. And her standing front flip is almost ready for competition.

"Since getting the new coach, we've all gotten better, don't you think?" asks Emilia. "Maybe we'll even beat Newport, so those snobs can go stick their noses somewhere else." Emilia laughs and punches the air. "Come on!" she calls, grabbing Nora's hand and dragging her into the gym.

Sven and Julia are already there. They coach gymnastics together. Julia is finishing high school right now, so she's been glad to have backup.

"Sven is a gymnastics world champion," she'd said when she introduced him to the team. She thought it was a huge honor that he agreed to coach her club and not Newport's, since they'd also wanted him.

Everyone thinks Sven is great. Nora, too, actually. But . . .

Great Talent

After they warm up, Julia claps her hands.
"We're going to practice front flips again!" she announces, and turns to Sven.
"Sven, do you mind taking over here? I need to sort something out quickly with my study group. I'll be right back."

Everyone jostles to get as close as possible to the front of the line. Nora dawdles, sliding farther and farther back. Maybe her turn won't come until Julia's back.

"What's wrong with you?" Emilia hisses. "Not up for it today?"

"Of course I am!" Nora grumbles. And she does want to do gymnastics, but . . .

She doesn't dare let herself think it, but the truth is that she doesn't like gymnastics so much when Sven helps.

He has such a strange approach to spotting her.
Nora doesn't like it. It doesn't feel right.
It feels like the touching they talked about in school,
the kind you don't have to put up with.

From anyone.

Actually, thinks Nora, she should say something. But there's no way that's what this is, right?

Sven's not just any adult. He's Sven. Who everyone thinks is great. The best coach they've ever had. Nice, and funny, too.

Besides, he said that she has great talent. He definitely won't say it again if she . . .

Such a Strange Feeling

"Nora?" That's his voice. She didn't even notice it was her turn. She lifts her foot to jump onto the mat. Oh no, now she's started off wrong. All right, one more time. Wrong again. Not that way. It's as if she doesn't know her own feet anymore.

She tries a third time. Still no good.

"What's the matter, Nora?" Sven asks. There's impatience in his tone. Everyone is looking at her. And she says it. Everything that's been on her mind. All of it.

Sven's jaw drops.

Okay, now it's out. Now what happens? She'd better go home immediately. Will she have to compete for Newport to keep doing gymnastics? Oh man, what a dumb thought.

Julia comes back into the gym. "It's good that you're here," says Sven. "I think we need to talk."

Suddenly, Nora finds herself alone. The others have taken a few steps back and look like they want nothing to do with the whole matter. Even Emilia isn't standing quite as close as she was just a moment ago.

Sven tells Julia the whole story. Nora only listens with half an ear. She wants the ground to swallow her. Julia and Sven fetch a few benches from the equipment room.

What is this supposed to mean?

"Would you all please come here?" Julia calls. "We have something to discuss." Nora bites her lip. Now this.

Nora Wants the Ground to Swallow Her

Murmuring and scraping feet. Why isn't there a hole in the gym floor? Nora wishes she had her hoodie; it's so easy to disappear into.

Julia wants to start talking, but Sven waves her off. He takes the floor.

Now he'll definitely say right away that spotting is necessary and completely different from how she perceives it. That he didn't know he was doing anything wrong. Nora tugs at her bodysuit but it's too tight to wrap herself in.

Sven clears his throat.

"That was very brave of you, Nora. Thank you very much," he says.

What now?

He explains that he's sorry, that he certainly didn't want his assistance to trigger such feelings in her. He says, "We'll have to find another solution," and asks if anyone else has felt uncomfortable.

No one comes forward.

Sven nods.

"This is a topic that's very important to me," he says. "I'll tell you why. You know that I started gymnastics really young. I had so much fun doing it. At least as much as Nora. And very quickly I became super good. Because of that, I enjoyed it even more. I loved how proud my dad was when I brought home a medal."

He continues: "I also had a super coach. He too was very proud of me and encouraged me to take on greater and greater challenges. And he thought . . ." Sven clears his throat. It sounds like he's finding it hard to keep talking.

"He thought that I was a particularly handsome boy. We always hugged whenever I did something especially good. I liked that."

Sven clears his throat. "But at some point, I started not liking it so much anymore. The hugs became too tight. Later, he would also embrace me in a strange way. Like we were . . . more than friends, more than Player and Coach. I thought it was awful, but I didn't say anything because I wasn't sure if I was just imagining it all. And I was scared that I'd no longer be his best and favorite gymnast that everyone was so proud of."

A Dark Cloud

Sven runs both hands over his face. Then he continues: "The touching got worse and more forceful. So bad that there no longer could be any doubt that this was not right. Illegal, even. I didn't dare do anything anymore because I thought it was my fault. After all, I didn't say anything when it started. I went on to win medals and was celebrated but wasn't really happy about it anymore. It was as if I was living in a dark cloud that I'd never find my way out from under."

"But you did find your way out," says Julia.
"Of the dark cloud, I mean."

Sven nods. "Yes, that's true. But it was a long road. At some point, I confided in my mother. She listened very calmly to everything and helped me. That coach is no longer allowed to work with children.
He got his due punishment."

He exhales deeply and squares his shoulders.

"I went to therapy, and it was made clear to me that a child is never to blame for these types of situations. It's great when someone is brave enough to address things directly, just like Nora did. But no child is obligated to or expected to do that. The adults who do these things are the ones responsible."

Pretty Brave

"It took me a long time to think about gymnastics with the same joy as before, but now I do again.
And to make sure it's the same for you, let's talk about how we can coach without making anyone feel uncomfortable. Maybe you can tell me how I can do better. Or would you rather that only Julia spot you? Whatever you decide is fine."

Emilia grabs Nora's hand and squeezes it tight. Nora pipes up. She says:

"Thanks, Sven. I think that you were pretty brave, too."

What We Want to Know

The team met again to discuss everything. A few kids who play other sports for the same club also joined them.

Julia thought of another important topic that should be discussed.

She is also a very good gymnast but can no longer participate in major competitions because she seriously injured herself once. And that happened because she totally overexerted herself. She desperately wanted to be the best. She's not at all sure if that was really her own idea. It could be that she only wanted it because it was so important to her mom.

Once the group started talking, they were amazed at what else they came up with.

They discussed each point in detail. And to be able to reflect back on their discussion later, they wrote down the most important things in a big, colorful list.

1. Abuse Prevention in Sports!

Sports are great. It's fun to train with others, especially when it's my favorite sport.

When we've succeeded, I feel it right down to my tiptoes.

Sometimes we hug each other out of sheer joy. But I don't have to receive hugs if I don't want to.

Even if I've found giving or receiving hugs nice before, I have the right not to like it next time and say so.

In sports, help is sometimes necessary.
I can say at any time that I'm not comfortable with touching. There's surely a way to do it differently. It's good to know in advance what physical contact is necessary.

I alone get to decide what happens to my body.

2. I Take Care of My Body

Sports are fun, even if they are strenuous.
And sometimes the strenuous part is the most fun.
But sometimes we do too much out of pure enthusiasm and ignore what our body is saying.

That's why we practice listening to it.
At the beginning of practice, we take time for a short session in which we say how our body feels right then.

3. I Do Sports Because I Want to and Not For Someone Else

We're a team, so we're there for each other. It's great that we can achieve a lot together.
But if I can't or don't want to do something, that's okay, too.

There are always days when I don't really feel up to things. That's normal. It's often the case that the fun comes back if I hold off for a little bit.

However, I can always consider whether the sport is still right for me. I don't have to hold out just because Mom or Dad or someone else might be sad if I stop.

I don't have to keep doing it because I already have all the equipment. Things can be resold.

But it's good to take my time when making a decision like this. Then I can be sure that I'm not just going through a little slump.

4. I Am Not Alone

Even if there's another reason I don't enjoy the sport as much anymore, I have the right to talk about it.

For example:

> The others always tease me.

> I get irritated because I'm not as good as the others.

> I get upset because I'm not that good, even though I actually like the sport.

The new coach is way too strict for me.

I'm afraid I'll always be last.

Someone teases me out of jealousy because I'm pretty good.

I feel totally uncomfortable in the new jerseys.

Since we only train for our next competition, I don't enjoy it so much anymore.

It's good to talk about it. No one has the right to bother me about it.

Maybe I'd like to talk to the whole group straight away, or maybe I'll find someone I trust to speak to by myself first.

We can then think together about what to do.

Sometimes it's good to get outside advice and help. There are experts you can turn to. It's perfectly fine to do that.

We take care of ourselves. Of our bodies. And of our good spirits.

Happy, uninjured athletes are always winners. Even when they lose the game, match, or competition.

Information Centers

U.S. Center for SafeSport
Main Line: (720) 531-0344
Reporting Line: (833) 5US-SAFE
www.maapp.uscenterforsafesport.org
Address: U.S. Center for SafeSport, P.O. Box 460308
Denver, CO 80246

SafeSport Helpline
Phone: (866) 200-0796
www.safesporthelpline.com

Canadian Centre for Ethics in Sport
Phone: (613) 521-3340
www.cces.ca/safesport
201-2723 Lancaster Rd.
Ottawa, ON K1B 0B1

Athletes Equity Resource Center
Email: AERCsports@gmail.com
www.athletesequityresourcecenter.com/athlete-assistance-program
1202 SW 17th Street , Suite 201
PMB 172, Ocala, FL, 34471

Little League Player Safety
www.littleleague.org/player-safety
Phone: (860) 585-4730

Child Welfare Information Gateway

Phone: (800) 394-3366

Email: info@childwelfare.gov

www.childwelfare.gov

National Child Abuse Hotline

Phone: (800) 422-4453

www.childhelphotline.org

National Council of Youth Sports

Phone: (470) 719-9091

www.ncys.org/safety

USA Gymnastics

response.resolution@usagym.org

www.usagym.org/safety/

Afterword

Sports are a great activity for young and old.

Above all, practicing and exercising as a group can be an enriching experience for children. They can try things out, test their limits, learn how to win and lose. Ideally, athletic training takes place in an empowering and safe environment. It helps to shape children into self-confident, healthy members of society.

In this book, Dagmar Geisler sensitively addresses a difficult topic and gives possible answers to the questions "What do I do, as a child, when something doesn't feel right?" and "How do I deal with suspected issues as a caregiver?" This book encourages children to pay attention to their feelings and to verbalize them, even in the context of sports. It sensitizes parents and caregivers to pay attention to the warning signs, to take statements seriously, and to intervene if they suspect something.

Medals are not more important than physical and mental health, especially not children's. Those who stand up for themselves always win in the end. It's important to teach this from an early age.

Alexandra Ndolo

About the Authors

Dagmar Geisler has already supported several generations of parents in guiding their children through emotionally difficult situations. Through her Safe Child, Happy Parent picture book series, the author sensitively covers the most important topics surrounding growing up: from body awareness to exploring your own emotional world to social interaction. Her work always includes a serving of humor. Especially when the topic is serious. Her books have been translated into twenty languages and also published in the United States.

Nikolai Renger was born in Karlsruhe and studied Visual Communication at the HFG in Pforzheim. He works as a freelance illustrator for various publishers and agencies and has been working at Atelier Remise in Karlsruhe since 2013.